Gloria!

Instrumental Solos for Easter

Arranged by Stephen Bulla

CURNOW MUSIC

EXCLUSIVELY DISTRIBUTED BY

HAL•LEONARD CORPORATION

7777 W. BLUEMOUND RD. P.O. BOX 13819 MILWAUKEE, WI 53213

Order Number: CMP 0529.01

Stephen Bulla
GLORIA!
B♭ Instruments (B♭ Clarinet, B♭ Trumpet and others)

ISBN 90-431-1117-1

CD number: 19.012-3 CMP
CD produced by: Stephen Bulla

Contents

Gloria!

Preface

This collection of familiar hymns has been chosen to be particularly appropriate for the Easter season. The selection reflects those songs that are widely used by churches at this time of year, and also a few that are simply related by their subject matter. It is hoped that all will present an enjoyable experience for soloist and listener alike.

The solos are arranged in a straightforward style, although frequent obligato and variation passages are interwoven with the familiar melodies to add interest. The range of difficulty is moderate, with the hope that the settings will provide something for everyone from novice to professional player.

With the accompaniment CD resource the soloist's musical experience will be enhanced for those occasions when an accompanist is not available. For the church musician, this collection, along with other CMP play-along publications such as 'Christmas Joy', 'Two for Christmas' and 'Great Hymns' presents ready-made material that will enhance every worship setting.

Stephen Bulla

Stephen Bulla received his degree in arranging and composition from Boston's Berklee College of Music, graduating Magna Cum Laude. Through his studies there, he developed an interest in the commercial music field, eventually leading to the present schedule of full-time composing and recording production.

In 1980 Mr. Bulla joined "The President's Own" U.S. Marine Band and White House Orchestra as Staff Arranger. As such, he is responsible for the production of music that encompasses many styles and instrumental combinations, most of which are performed for Presidential functions and visiting dignitaries. His musical arrangements for many performers, including Sarah Vaughan, The Manhattan Transfer, Mel Torme, and Doc Severinsen, were featured on the PBS television series "In Concert at the White House." He has also produced orchestrations for Marvin Hamlisch, Joe Raposo, and jazz pianist Dick Hyman.

A variety of free-lance commercial projects find Mr. Bulla in the studio producing new recordings, including the popular "Spiritual to the Bone" series of jazz trombone ensemble CDs. In 1990 he was awarded the prestigious ADDY Award for best original music/TV spot, and recently he provided the music score for the "Century of Flight" series on the Discovery Channel.

In 1998 he was honored by The Salvation Army in New York for his extensive contribution to their musical repertoire. This event included a "Profile" concert of his compositions, featuring performances by the New York Staff Band.

His commissioned concert works include instrumental compositions that are performed and recorded internationally. The Dutch, British, and New Zealand Brass Band Championship organizations have all commissioned test pieces from his pen. His wind band compositions are published by Curnow Music Press and De Haske Music Publications.

Stephen Bulla is a member of ASCAP (American Society of Composers, Authors, and Publishers) and has received that organization's Performance Award annually since 1984.

With a growing catalog of works published and recorded in the U.S. and abroad, Mr. Bulla travels frequently as a guest conductor, adjudicator, and clinician.

GLORIA!
Instrumental Solos for Easter
(with Piano Accompaniment)

TRACK 3

Christ the Lord is Risen Today

From Lyra Davidica (1708)
Arr. by **Stephen Bulla** (ASCAP)

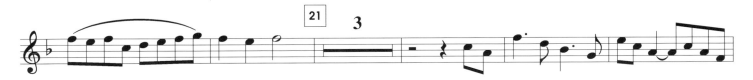

B♭ Instruments (B♭ Clarinet,
B♭ Trumpet and others)

Christ Arose

Robert Lowry (1826-1899)
Arr. by **Stephen Bulla** (ASCAP)

Come Thou Almighty King

TRACK 5

Felice de Giardini (1716-1796)
Arr. by **Stephen Bulla** (ASCAP)

B♭ Instruments (B♭ Clarinet,
B♭ Trumpet and others)

Crown Him with Many Crowns

G.J. Elvey (1816-1893)
Arr. by **Stephen Bulla** (ASCAP)

9

B♭ Instruments (B♭ Clarinet,
B♭ Trumpet and others)

Come, Ye Faithful

Sir Arthur S. Sullivan (1842-1900)
Arr. by **Stephen Bulla** (ASCAP)

TRACK 8

Golden Harps are Sounding

(Tune: Hermas)

Frances Havergal (1836-1879)
Arr. by **Stephen Bulla** (ASCAP)

11

Bb Instruments (Bb Clarinet,
Bb Trumpet and others)

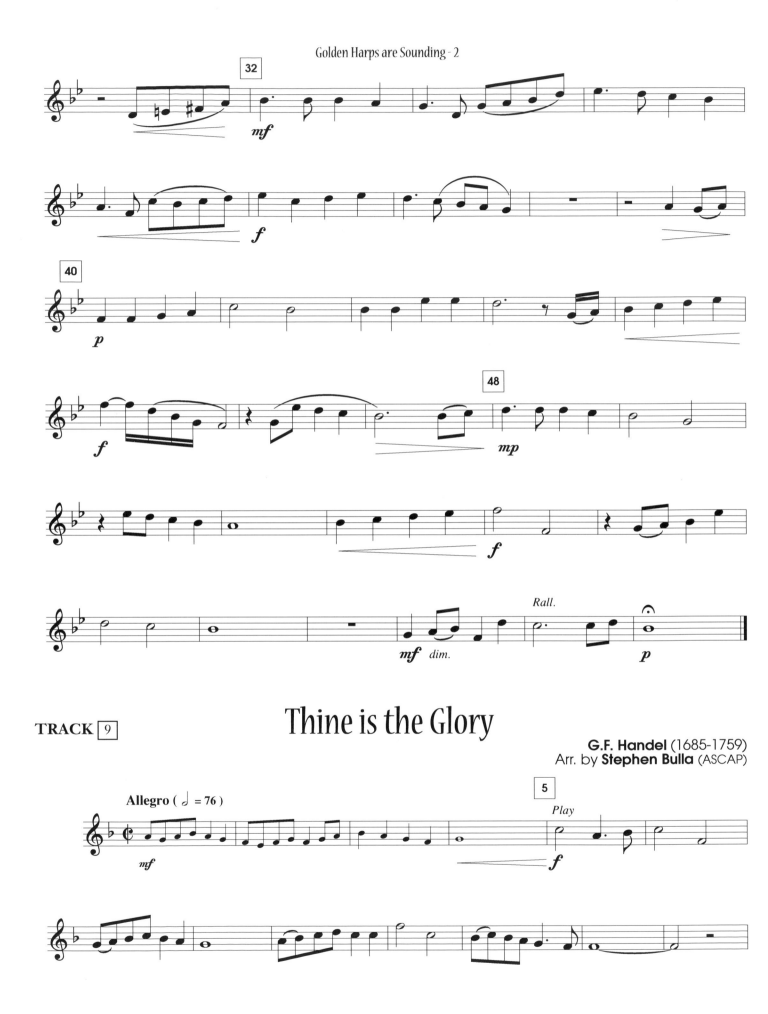

TRACK 9

Thine is the Glory

G.F. Handel (1685-1759)
Arr. by **Stephen Bulla** (ASCAP)

B♭ Instruments (B♭ Clarinet,
B♭ Trumpet and others)

Passion Chorale

J.S. Bach
Arr. by **Stephen Bulla** (ASCAP)

At the Cross

Ralph E. Hudson (1843-1901)
Arr. by **Stephen Bulla** (ASCAP)

15

Bb Instruments (Bb Clarinet,
Bb Trumpet and others)

Were You There?

American Spiritual
Arr. by **Stephen Bulla** (ASCAP)

Copyright © 2001 by Curnow Music Press, Inc.